Savitri's Three Wishes

A myth from India

Chapter 1

A gift from the goddess

There was once a great king who had far-reaching lands, many wives, immense palaces and treasure-houses stuffed with gold and jewels. But he had no children. Not one. He longed for a child.

Every day, morning and evening, he prayed to the gods and goddesses. 'I will live like a hermit on rice and water, though I am a king, if you give me a child, give me one child.'

He kept his promise. He had his silks, jewels and chains of gold packed away. Instead, he wore the plainest, roughest clothes. He ate little, only rice and vegetables.

For drink, he took only water. Every day, at his

• *Savitri:* (say) 'sah-veet-ree'.　　**3**

palace gates, food was handed out to those who had none. Shoes were given to those whose shoes were worn out. Clothes were given to the ragged.

At last, the goddess Savitri appeared to him. 'I shall send you a child,' she said, 'as a reward for your kindness and humility.'

The King knelt and thanked her, calling her a gracious goddess, a merciful goddess ...

'Hush!' she said. 'Listen to me. You want a child and you shall have a child. I warn you though, when you have your wish, do not complain. You shall have a daughter. Do not dare to say that you want a son!'

'I am only thankful, great goddess,' said the King. 'Send me a daughter, and she shall be my greatest treasure. I shall call her Savitri, in your honour.'

A goddess keeps her word. That same day, the King's favourite wife came to him and told him she was with child. The King was speechless with joy.

The King too, kept his word. When his child

was at last born, he named her Savitri, and he adored her. He was enchanted by her little face and her tiny hands, and by how tightly her tiny fingers could grip his  large finger. He could hardly keep from the Queen's rooms, where his ministers would find him singing to the baby, or holding bright flowers for her to clutch at.

As Savitri grew, the King delighted in her company, and he raised her to live as he did. She was dressed in plain clothes and she ate plain food. Every day the King told her stories. She sat in his lap and listened with her eyes fixed on his face.

When she was older, the King had her taught to read and write and sent for the best teachers of mathematics. She learned about other countries, and about history and wars.

'She is to be my only child,' said the King. 'She must be taught these things, so she can rule this land after I am dead.'

Blessed by a goddess, and loved by her father, Savitri grew into a beautiful young woman. Anyone who spoke with her soon found that she was as clever as she was beautiful. Yet no princes came to ask for her hand in marriage. Many princes wanted a pretty wife, but few wanted one so beautiful that she made them nervous. And hardly any princes wanted a wife more intelligent and educated than they were themselves.

'Father,' Savitri said. 'I shall never have a husband if I wait here for one to come to me. I must go out and find a husband.'

So Savitri left her father's palace to search for a husband. She travelled in a

howdah, high on the back of an elephant. Soldiers walked and rode with her, to protect her from robbers.

Behind them came ox-carts, full of food, and gifts for the people she would meet. There were clothes of silk and jewels, too. When Savitri met other kings and queens, she had to dress like a princess.

Behind the ox-carts came many servants, some walking, some riding – servants to look after the clothes, servants to cook the food, servants to look after the animals and servants to repair the carts if they broke. It was as if Savitri led an army.

Chapter 2
Prince Satyavan

Savitri visited many, many cities and many royal
palaces, and she met scores of princes. Dressed in
her silks and jewels, she was dazzlingly beautiful,
as beautiful as the goddess whose name she had.
The princes she met all thought her beautiful,
but none of them wanted to marry her.

'She is too beautiful,' they said to their
mothers and fathers. 'And she is ill-natured!
She told me I was wrong!'

• *Satyavan:* (say) 'suht-yah-vuhn'.   **9**

Savitri didn't care. She thought the princes were strutting and boastful, but not well educated. They dressed in silks, gold, pearls and peacock feathers and sneered when she said she usually wore plain clothes of cotton. When she asked them about the people who grew their food, they laughed and said they knew nothing of poor people.

Savitri continued on her travels. She came to a hermitage, a place where a holy man had made his home, and lived a quiet, plain life. Others had come there to share his peace, and they made travellers welcome. Savitri was happy to live quietly, so she decided to stay there for a while with all her people and rest. She went into the temple-hall in the hermitage and spoke to the eldest teacher, begging his permission to stay in the guest house there. The teacher said that all travellers were welcome. While they were talking, a young man came into the hall, leading a frail old man by the arm.

The teacher saw that Savitri watched them.

He explained, 'The old man is King Dyumatsena, who has lost his kingdom. He lives here with us.'

'Is he blind?' Savitri asked. It seemed to her, from the way the old man moved, that he had difficulty seeing things.

'He is,' said the teacher.

'His servant is so careful with him,' Savitri said, 'and so kind.'

'That is not his servant, but his son, Prince Satyavan. The Prince loves his father, it is true.'

Savitri stayed at the hermitage for some weeks. She watched Satyavan with his father. He was never impatient or unkind with the old man. He was kind to other people too. He was always ready to help them with their work, and he always spoke to everyone and smiled. She saw that everyone liked him.

Savitri spoke to Satyavan herself and found that he was clever and funny. She felt that he liked her. One day, when they had been laughing together, she said, 'Tell me, Satyavan, do you ever plan to marry?'

• *Dyumatsena:* (say) 'd-yoo-muht-seh-nu'.

'Where will I find a wife?' he said. 'I am a prince without a kingdom! My father will be unhappy if I marry a poor woman, but no princess would have me.'

'There is a princess sitting beside you who would gladly marry you, if you would take her,' Savitri said. Satyavan stared at her in surprise and she smiled. She told him about her life and why she was on this journey. 'I have met many rich princes who would not marry me because they fear I am cleverer than they are. They were proud and boastful and boring. You are none of those things. But perhaps you, too, think I am too clever?'

'I love your quick mind,' he said. 'I would think myself blessed to have you as my wife. But your father will think I am marrying you for his kingdom.'

'My father trusts my judgement a little better than that,' she said. 'I shall go home, and tell him about you, and we shall see.'

So she returned to her father's palace.

Her father was glad to see her again. 'Did you find yourself a husband?' he asked.

'I did. I shall marry Prince Satyavan.'

Her father sent at once for his royal astrologer, and asked the man to draw up Satyavan's horoscope.

'It is already done,' the man said. 'We astrologers draw up the charts of all royal babies when they are born. If you will excuse me for a short while, I will find the chart and bring it to you.'

Savitri and her father had much to talk about after her long journey. They sat in the shade and ate mango until the astrologer returned. He did not look happy.

'What is the matter?' Savitri asked.

'Oh, Princess, the news is not good. The man you have chosen is a fine man – but it is written in the patterns of the stars that he will die in a year's time.'

The King and Savitri were shocked. But then Savitri asked calmly, 'Does Satyavan know this?'

'I think not,' said the astrologer. 'The King, his father, lost his kingdom just after Satyavan's birth. They may not have seen a chart of his birth and fate.'

Savitri said, 'Good. We must be married as soon as can be.'

'What?' cried her father. 'You must not be married to him at all!'

'I have met many men,' said Savitri. 'From them I have chosen Satyavan. I did not choose carelessly, and I do not dither and swither and change my mind every moment. I shall marry Satyavan or no one.'

'But, Daughter, I cannot bear you to suffer a marriage so soon followed by a funeral. You are young, and have known little sadness as yet. Can you imagine how much pain this will cause you?'

'I have had a safe and happy life, it is true,' Savitri said. 'But even I know that we cannot be happy every hour of every day. If I run along a garden path for sheer happiness, I may trip and hurt my head and knees.' She laughed. 'This is life, Father. It cannot be helped. We must simply face it with courage. Read my horoscope, and surely you will see this marriage written there. I have made my choice. I shall not change. If one year with Satyavan is all I may have, then I will seize it. Don't waste effort in trying to change my mind.'

The King saw that nothing could do that. 'Then we must arrange the wedding as soon as possible.'

'It won't take long,' Savitri said. 'There is no need for great feasts or show. Satyavan and I are used to living simply. A little honey on our rice and we will think it a feast! But may I ask one

favour, Father?'

'My dear one, ask anything.'

'Say nothing to anyone about Satyavan's fate.
If he doesn't know, let him remain unknowing.'

The King agreed. Soon a great troop of soldiers and elephants left the palace, carrying the King and Savitri back to the hermitage. Satyavan was joyful when he was told that he and Savitri would be married the very next day, but his father, the blind King, had doubts. 'Life with my son, here in the hermitage, will not be like life in a royal palace,' he said. 'Can you live like us, Savitri?'

'I have never lived a life of riches, even though I am a princess,' she said. 'If I can be with Satyavan, I shall be happy.'

The next day they were married and began their life together.

Chapter 3
One year later

Savitri kept her word. Her clothes were the simplest and plainest she could wear. She ate nothing but rice, fruit and vegetables; and she drank only water. She cooked for her husband and father-in-law, tended the fire, swept the floor, fetched water, and did everything that was needful without complaint. Nor did she ever mention what she knew about the shortness of Satyavan's life.

At first she hardly thought of it herself. A year seemed a long time.

She and Satyavan rose together in the morning, worked together, laughed and talked together, and went to the same bed at night. They were happy.

When three months had passed, it still seemed that their time would last for always, and they were happier than ever.

Then six months had passed, and Savitri realised that half their time had gone. Still, six months was twenty-six weeks, or one hundred and eighty-three days. That was still a long time, surely?

But another three months passed, leaving only three more, and that didn't seem so long ...

Three months became two months ...

Two months became one month. Then three weeks. Then two weeks. Now all the time they had spent together seemed so short.

Savitri prayed to all the gods. She prayed to her own special goddess, Savitri. She asked them all to change her husband's fate and let him live.

But Satyavan's death was written in the stars.

Can even the gods change
the circling of the stars
above us?

Three days before
Satyavan was to die, Savitri
vowed to fast and pray for
all that time, both day and
night. At least she hoped she
would gain strength to endure
the sorrow she must suffer.

The last day of Satyavan's life came. Nothing
could stop it. That morning, Satyavan was
readying himself to go to the forest, to collect
wood. Savitri came from the temple, where she
had been praying all night. She knelt before her
father-in-law, and asked him if she might go
with Satyavan.

'Why?' he asked, surprised. 'That is not work
for you, and you work harder than anyone could
ask already.'

'You should go and sleep,' Satyavan said. 'You
have been awake all night.'

'If you are happy with my work,' Savitri said, 'then please grant me this one small favour. Let me spend this day with Satyavan, wherever he goes.'

'If that is what you wish,' said her father-in-law. 'Go with him, Daughter, and my blessing will be with you both.'

So Satyavan and Savitri went to the forest together.

Satyavan gathered wood for a short while, but as his bundle grew heavy, he felt dizzy and weak, and fell to his knees. Savitri ran to him. Satyavan said, 'Let me put my head in your lap. I shall feel better soon.'

So she knelt, and let him lie with his head in her lap. She stroked his head, but looked sharply about her. So keenly did she look that she saw Lord Yama coming to them. Lord Yama, who is Death.

Satyavan breathed his last breath and his soul rose from his body. Lord Yama caught it by the hand, and led it away.

Savitri gently laid her husband's head on the ground. Then she followed Lord Yama and Satyavan's soul.

Lord Yama heard footsteps behind him, and turned. 'Savitri!' he said. 'Why do you follow me?'

'I follow my husband, Lord.'

'You cannot. Go back to the living. Don't fear for your husband. He was a good man and will know great happiness in my kingdom.'

'Great Lord Yama,' Savitri said, 'I know that you mean us no ill. It is the law that all must die, and it is the law that you must gather the souls into your kingdom. All must obey the law. I honour you, Great Lord Yama, for doing your duty. But I, too, have a duty and I must obey it. I have taken Satyavan as my husband so my place is at his side, I must and shall follow him. Satyavan is also my dear friend, and friends must be loyal to one another. So I must and shall follow my dear friend, Satyavan.'

'A fine speech,' said Lord Yama. 'You have a character as beautiful as your face. But still, you may not come with me, Savitri. If you will turn back to the living, I will grant you a wish, any wish.' But then, as she opened her mouth, he said, 'Any wish except the life of your husband!'

'Thank you, Great Lord,' Savitri said. 'I beg you will give my father-in-law back his sight.'

'It is done,' said Lord Yama.

In the hermitage the old King cried aloud as

colour flashed on his blind eyes. He pressed his
hands to them and then took them away. He
saw people moving. He saw green leaves. He saw
a woman in a yellow sari carrying a blue pot.
Savitri's first wish was fulfilled.

Lord Yama went on, following the path to his Kingdom of Death. Savitri still followed him. The road became rough and edged with thorns. Soon Savitri's clothes hung in strips and rags, torn by the thorns. Her arms and legs bled from scratches. 'Savitri! Go home now!' said Lord Yama. 'I granted you a wish.'

'We must all obey the law,' said Savitri. 'You obey when you come to take our souls away. And I wish to obey you, Great Lord – truly, I would obey you, but there is a greater and more unbreakable law than yours, which I must obey first.'

'What law can be greater than mine?' asked Lord Yama.

'The law of my heart, Lord, which says that I cannot turn away from my husband because my clothes are a little torn. My heart's law, which says I cannot leave a friend's side because I bleed a little. I must come with you.'

'Savitri, you speak beautiful words. I will grant you a second wish. Anything – ah, but not your husband's life!'

'I do not ask it, Great Lord. You have your duty. I would not ask you to break it. Instead, please grant my father many children. I am his only child, and I know he loves me as much as a man can love a child, but he wished for many children, and I know he would love them all.'

'You wish for others and not for yourself,' said Lord Yama.

'These wishes are for myself. If my father and my father-in-law are happy, then I am happy indeed.'

'Your wish is granted,' said Lord Yama. 'Now go home!'

Far away, in the palace of Savitri's father, his wives formed a queue outside his door. One by one they went inside and told him that they were expecting a child. The King laughed and cried, he was so happy.

Chapter 4
The final wish

Lord Yama went on his way to the Kingdom of
Death. The road climbed a steep hill. Lord Yama
looked back and saw Savitri still following. Now
she was so exhausted that she scrambled up the
hill almost on hands and knees. Her hair was
wild and tangled, she was covered in dust, her
clothes were in tatters and she bled.

Lord Yama stopped. 'Savitri, now I order you
to go home.'

'Lord, I cannot. I shall not.'

'Savitri, your courage and determination are admirable. But you are alive and must go back to the living.'

'I will not.'

'What if I grant you one last wish – something for yourself this time. But not the life of your husband.'

'I promise I will never ask for that, Lord.'

'But do you promise that you will go home if I grant you this last wish?'

'If you grant me this wish in full, Lord, I will go home, I promise.'

'But you must not ask for the life of your husband.'

'I will not, Lord.'

'Then tell me, what is your wish?'

'I wish for myself many children, Lord!'

'A good wish and –'

'I have not finished, Lord! I wish for many children, and I wish their father to be Satyavan.'

'Oh.' Lord Yama sat down on the path to think. He thought for a long time. He thought about all sides of the problem.

Savitri sat down with him and waited.

'You have not asked for the life of your husband,' he said.

'No, Lord.'

'But I promised, to grant your wish, and I must grant it, on my honour as a god.'

'Yes, Lord.'

'I promised to grant you whatever you asked, if it was not your husband's life.'

'That's right, Lord.'

'And you asked for many children, and for their father to be Satyavan.'

'That is what I asked, Lord.'

'But Satyavan is dead, and he cannot father children if he is dead.'

'That is so, Lord.'

'Then what am I to do, Savitri?'

'You are the Great Lord Yama. You know what you have to do.'

Lord Yama thought some more, and then he said, 'I think you are a clever woman, Savitri, and

I think you have caught me in a trap.'

'I would never do that, Lord.'

'But I cannot see how I can keep my promise unless I return Satyavan to life. Can you?'

'He must be alive to father children, Lord, that is true.'

'I could break my promise, Savitri.'

'The Great Lord Yama, who treats kings and poor alike, would never break his promise,' Savitri said.

'No, I shall not,' said Lord Yama, and he released the hand of Satyavan's soul. 'You have won back your husband's life, Savitri. I am thankful that there are few with your courage.'

Then Savitri blinked and she was in the forest, with Satyavan's head in her lap. Satyavan was yawning and opening his eyes, as if he'd been asleep. He smiled at Savitri and got to his feet, ready to carry home the wood. Then he said, 'What have you been doing? Your clothes are rags and you're bleeding!'

'I fell among thorns,' she said.

'I told you to stay at home,' he said. 'Carry that light bundle – we'll go home and you can wash and change.'

So they went home to the hermitage – and found Satyavan's father

running about everywhere and looking at everything. He had been blind for so long that the sight of a footprint in dust, a bowl of milk, a lamp's flame, were all wonderful things to him.

Then an invitation came from Savitri's father, asking them to go and stay with him, to celebrate the birth of Savitri's many younger brothers and sisters. They did go. Seeing her father so happy made Savitri happy indeed.

Afterwards, Savitri and Satyavan returned to the hermitage, and lived together contentedly for many years. They had many sons and many daughters.

At the end of their long lives, neither Savitri nor Satyavan had to know the pain of losing the other because Lord Yama came for them on the same night. He led them away together and they walked behind him, hand in hand, into his Kingdom of Death.

Orpheus and Eurydice

A myth from Ancient Greece

Chapter 1

Orpheus and his lyre

Orpheus was the finest musician and singer who ever lived. His playing and singing were so beautiful that Apollo himself, the god of the sun and music, came down from Mount Olympus and gave Orpheus his own lyre. 'You will make greater music on it than I can,' said the god.

When Orpheus played on that lyre, he could make the sad happy, and the happy sad. He could make his listeners drowse and sleep, if he chose.

When he played, the birds perched on his shoulders to hear, the sheep gathered near to listen. Wild animals, even fierce lions and wolves, crept close to him and lay down to listen with their heads on their paws. So powerful was his music that, to hear it, rocks rolled after him, and trees tugged their roots from the ground and followed him.

Wherever Orpheus went, people gathered around in crowds to hear him play and sing.

Whole villages, whole towns were left with empty streets while Orpheus sang. Among the people who went to hear him sing was Eurydice. She heard him, and she loved him. Once she'd heard him sing, she couldn't go home, but followed him wherever he went, over mountains and through forests.

Orpheus loved Eurydice too. Once he'd found her, he played no sad music. They married, and their wedding was attended by singing birds and walking trees, by laughing people, howling wolves and dancing stones. For a year Orpheus and Eurydice were never apart and always happy. At the end of that year, Eurydice was following Orpheus across a meadow, when she trod on a snake. It bit her and she died.

All that was left of her was buried in the earth. Her spirit, the soul of her, had gone into the Underworld, the kingdom of the god Hades and his sad wife, Persephone.

No one who had gone to the Underworld had ever returned.

• *Hades:* (say) 'hay-deez'.
• *Persephone:* (say) 'per-sef-oh-nee'.

37

Orpheus played no sad music then, either. Without Eurydice, he played no music at all.

He hardly ate. He no longer washed or changed his clothes. He became dirty and ragged. He left his hair and beard uncombed, so they grew long, tangled and wild. All day long, every day, he tried to understand that he would never see Eurydice again. However hard he tried, it made no sense to him. He tried to think what he would do, now he was without her, but nothing seemed worth doing.

All he wanted was to be with her again. So all he could do was go down into the Underworld and ask its king, Hades, to let Eurydice go.

He knew that Hades had never released any of the souls he ruled. He knew that the journey to the Underworld was dangerous for the living. But he hated being without Eurydice. Going to the Underworld was easier than suffering another day without her.

Orpheus took no food or drink with him – he couldn't think of things like that. He could think

of nothing but finding Eurydice. Dirty, ragged,
hungry, sleepless, he walked south. He walked
for days, crossing rivers, climbing forested
mountains. When he stopped, exhausted, the
birds brought him nuts and berries. Lions
brought him lambs to eat. The birds and animals
knew him, and hoped he would play his lyre for
them again, if they kept him alive. He played to
reward them, but the music was so sad that the
wolves howled and the lions wept.

Chapter 2

Journey to the Underworld

Orpheus reached the cave that led into the Underworld. The way was narrow, cold and dark. Down, down, down and colder than winter. Down, down and further down, with the weight of the whole Earth hanging above his head.

The air was colder still, chilled with water and

he smelt the stink of the river Styx. The waters of the Styx are black, cold and poisonous. It cannot be waded, or swum, but it must be crossed to reach the Underworld.

All who reach its banks must be rowed across by the ferryman, Charon, and he must be paid. That is why pennies are placed on the eyes of the dead before they are buried, and sometimes in their mouths. When their ghosts reach the Styx, they can use the pennies to pay the ferryman.

Some of the dead are not given pennies – either because they die alone, or because their families are too poor. These ghosts are trapped on the banks of the river Styx. They cannot go back, because they are dead and no longer have a place in the world of the living. They cannot go forward because Charon will not take them across the river if they cannot pay him.

Orpheus heard these ghosts before he reached them. He heard the murmuring and sobbing of their voices as they begged and pleaded, endlessly, to be taken across the river.

Then he came among them, and they crowded about him. Their breath and their touch was icy. They clutched at his clothes, at his hair, at his beard, at his arms. They were behind him, in front of him, beside him – he couldn't escape them. They pressed themselves against him, because they smelled his warm blood and

envied it. Blood is life, and the ghosts longed for life.

'Please,' they said, 'oh, please –'

Whispering.

'Help us. Please.'

Clutching.

'Give us blood.'

'Please, oh please –'

'Give us money. Please.'

'I have no money,' Orpheus said. 'I cannot give you blood.'

They didn't listen to him. Some were transparent, they'd been there so long, fading away. They longed to cross the river.

'Please, oh please ... Help us, please ... Give us blood. Please, please ...'

Instead, Orpheus unslung his bag from his shoulder. From it, he took his lyre. He sat down among the whispering, clutching, pleading ghosts, and he played. At first they crowded round him, not listening, desperate to leave that place. Pulling at him, sniffing at him.

But slowly, the music reached them. Little by little, they heard and listened. The constant sound of the ghosts' sobbing and pleading had gone on for ever, like the sound of waves against a beach. Now they listened to the music they had loved when they had lived, and they were soothed. Many lay down and slept, for the first time in all the centuries since they had been there and their moaning finally faded away.

Orpheus stood and, still playing, walked through them to the river's edge.

There was Charon's ferry-boat, a ghost of a boat, a rotting hulk. Charon stood in it. He was as thin as bones, and grey. Unsmiling, he watched Orpheus. 'You have no business here,' he said.

'I must cross to the other side,' Orpheus said.

'You are alive.'

'But Eurydice – she is over there. I must be with her.'

'Your time to cross the river will come,' Charon said.

'But when?' Orpheus cried. 'In a year? Ten years? Twenty? I can't be without her. I must go to join her.'

Charon laughed and held out his hand.

'I have no money,' Orpheus said.

'Then you stay here,' Charon said. 'With them.'

'Please take me across, please –'

'Now you sound like them,' Charon said.

'I'll play for you,' Orpheus said. His music had calmed the ghosts: perhaps it could please the ferryman ... He ran his fingers over the strings, making a sound like clear, sweet water – very different from the water of the Styx.

'No lullabies will charm me,' Charon said.

Orpheus played no lullabies. He played a dance tune, bright and quick and light. Charon twisted his mouth and turned his face away, scorning it. But he soon turned his head again. He listened. The music, so lovely in that cold place, made his heart ache. When the music stopped, he said, 'If I row you across, will you play for me again?'

Orpheus nodded.

'Get in,' Charon said. 'You have your passage.'

Orpheus climbed into the half-ruined boat, and Charon took up the oars. He rowed Orpheus across the cold, stinking waters to the other side.

Orpheus jumped from the boat and climbed the bank.

Charon shouted after him, 'You said you would play for me again!' His voice echoed from cavern walls far away.

'I shall come back,' Orpheus said, 'bringing Eurydice with me. Then I will play for you again.'

Charon slumped over his oars. 'Hades will never let her go. He is jealous of everything that is his. He will keep you. Play now – keep your promise. You will never come back this way.'

'When I return,' Orpheus said, and went on into the darkness.

Chapter 3

A deal with Hades

From ahead, from the darkness, came a wild barking. It echoed around the caverns. Orpheus stood still, afraid. The barking was that of a pack of dogs, of wild, hungry, fierce dogs, the kind that attacked travellers on lonely roads.

From the darkness sprang one dog, one huge dog. It came at Orpheus, baying. It had three heads, and the lashing scaly tail of a great snake. This was Cerberus, the dog that guarded Hades' kingdom.

• *Cerberus:* (say) 'sur-ber-uss'.

Orpheus had faced many wild, fierce creatures. Now, as often before, he played on his lyre. He played smooth, flowing music that fell on Cerberus' ears like soft rain.

Cerberus had never heard such sounds. The great dog had heard the cries and moans of ghosts, the splashes of Charon's rowing, dismal echoes ... But such music it had never heard. It stopped, astonished.

Orpheus walked closer, still playing. Cerberus growled, but let him come nearer.

Orpheus knelt beside the hound and played lullabies and sad, sweet laments. The great, fierce, three-headed hound whimpered, lay down, and then rolled on his back. From three fanged mouths lolled three tongues. The great hound fell asleep.

Orpheus rubbed the hound's belly. Then
he rose and went on into the Underworld. He
entered Hades' dark, chill hall. In silence, he
walked to the foot of Hades' throne.

There sat glowering Hades. Beside him sat his
wife, the beautiful, sad Persephone, who longs
always for the bright world above.

Orpheus knelt and waited for the King of the
Underworld to give him permission to speak.

'You are alive,' Hades said, at last. 'I know, by
the din your footsteps made. Why are you here?'

'To ask a favour, great King,' Orpheus said.

Hades laughed. 'I grant no favours to the living.'

Persephone leaned forward and spoke. 'What is it you would ask?'

'Eurydice, my dear Eurydice, is here in your Hall, great Queen ...'

The Queen was puzzled. 'Yes. But what would you ask?'

'Let her go, Queen – let her go!'

Hades laughed again, and the Queen said, 'My husband allows none to go. If your Eurydice is here, here she must stay. And you must go back to the world above.' The Queen's voice broke, because the world above was where she wanted to be. For six long months of every year, when she had to live in her husband's cold Underworld, she longed for light, sun and warmth.

Orpheus sobbed. 'No, Queen – no. Not without her. I cannot be without her. I cannot go back and leave her here in the dark and cold. Please, I beg you, please, let her go.'

The Queen looked at Hades, but Hades shook his head. 'All the gold in the earth, all the silver held tight in stone – it belongs to me,' he said. 'All the iron, all the copper – it belongs to me. Every diamond, ruby, emerald, sapphire – I grasp them hard. If you would have them, then you must sweat for them. All the dead too, are mine. I hold hard to what I have. I give nothing away. Eurydice is mine.'

'You want me to work for her?' Orpheus said. 'You want me to pay? I can pay with music. I'll play for you.'

'I want none of your noise,' Hades said.

But Persephone said, 'Play, please play. Play me something the shepherds play when it's hot and the flocks are drowsing.'

Orpheus played. He played the shepherds' music and Persephone leaned forward to listen. Her eyes opened wide, then they filled with tears, so much did she long for the land above. Although hearing the music hurt, it soothed too. She wept to hear it, but was glad to weep.

Hades scowled. The music didn't move him. He shook his head.

Orpheus played a lament for his loss of Eurydice. He shed no tears. The lyre sobbed instead. Hades' hard face softened. The sobbing and moaning of the lost dead was with him always. He hardened himself against them and didn't hear them.

But he heard the music. It spoke to him for the dead. In the music, he heard their sorrow and their longing. 'Stop playing,' Hades said.

'Go on, go on,' said Persephone.

Orpheus played on. From every part of the
Underworld, the ghosts came. They gathered
about Hades' throne, silent, staring, listening
and longing.

Some remembered music played before kings
in firelit halls. Others remembered tunes at a
village wedding, or pipe music in a market place.
But all remembered and all ached.

Orpheus lifted his head and saw Eurydice
looking at him. He stopped playing.
The lyre hung from his hand.

Eurydice stood among the
other grey ghosts beside
Hades' throne. A moan rose
from the others. They cried,
they whispered, because the
music had stopped.

'Play again!' Hades said.

'Let Eurydice go,' Orpheus said.

'Play.'

'Let her go.'

'If you play again, I'll let her go.'

Shrieks burst from the ghosts.

Shrieks and cries because Eurydice was to be set free, but they were not. Then there were moans and pleas for the music to begin again.

'Promise,' Orpheus said. 'Give me your word that you will let her go.'

'My word,' Hades said. 'I give you my word, on my honour as a god, that if you play again, I will let Eurydice go.'

Orpheus played again. The ghosts wept bitter tears, hearing that music and knowing they would never hear such music again. They did not want it to end.

But music must end. Orpheus stopped playing and held out his hand to Eurydice. She stepped forward to take it.

Then Hades said, 'I will let Eurydice go – but you must not look at her until she stands in the sunlight.'

Orpheus dropped his hand and looked at Hades. 'Great King, you gave your word.'

Hades smiled. 'I keep my word. If you can climb back to the upper world, and never once look behind you, never once look at Eurydice until she stands under the sun – then she may return to the living. Yet if you once look – if you glance – behind, then she is still mine.'

Orpheus looked at Persephone, but she shook her head. 'He is King here,' she said.

Orpheus said to Eurydice, 'Follow me. I shall not look back.'

Chapter 4
Don't look back

Orpheus walked out of Hades' hall, his back stiff, his eyes staring before him. But his eyes saw nothing. The only thing he wanted to see was behind him. All he thought was: is she behind me?

He knew that she must be. He had asked her to follow him, and no one would want to stay in Hades' hall. She was as silent as a ghost, unspeaking, her footsteps unheard, but for sure she was behind him.

He came down by the stinking shores of the Styx, and there lay Cerberus, still sleeping. Orpheus passed the hound quietly. Eurydice, behind him, made no sound.

Orpheus had to stop himself from turning his head. He had to believe that she was behind him.

At the bank of the Styx, there was the half-wrecked boat. The ferryman sat in it, waiting. As soon as he saw Orpheus, he called out to him.

'Play again! You promised you would play again!'

'I will,' Orpheus said. 'But please, ferryman, tell me – is there a woman behind me? Does she follow me?'

Charon peered into the darkness behind Orpheus. 'I see no one.'

Orpheus' head started to turn, but he clenched his teeth and stiffened his muscles. He would not look behind. 'Look carefully ... My wife ... Does she follow me? Does she?'

'A ghost, is she? Ghosts are hard to see. They're grey, faint ... She could be there and I'd never see her. Ah, no!' He held out his oar to stop Orpheus stepping into the boat. 'Play first. You promised you would play again.'

Orpheus lifted his lyre and played again. As he played, he listened, trying to hear the slightest sound behind him. He thought his right side grew colder than the rest of him – was that because she had come close, to listen? Or, in the deep chill of the Underworld, was it only that he wished for her to be at his side?

He finished the music and stepped into Charon's boat. He held his breath, waiting to feel the boat rock as she stepped aboard – but a ghost has no weight.

Charon started to row. 'Play as we cross. I never hear such music.'

So Orpheus played and sang – a song that he knew Eurydice used to love. He hoped that she smiled as she listened, but he didn't dare turn his head to see.

Charon rowed slowly, but he kept his word. He carried Orpheus to the other side, and watched him step from the boat.

'Play one more time,' Charon said. 'Once more.'

'It's a long way, back to the world above,' protested Orpheus.

'But I must stay here for ever, and it may be long before I hear you play again.'

So Orpheus played one last time, and he kept his eyes on Charon and the boat. Then he said, 'Follow me,' though he didn't look behind. He walked away from the Styx, climbing up through the caverns. With every step he paused, listening. He tipped his head backwards, listening. Was she there?

He started to turn his head – but stopped himself. He must believe she was there, but not look. When he reached the upper world, when they both stood under the sun again, then he could look at her until the sun went down. They would live their lives, and every day of their lives, he could look at her.

It was a long hard climb. It's easy to tell of such a climb, but hard to do it. Step by step Orpheus climbed, out of death, until he saw sunlight shining on a wall.

The mouth of the cave was near. He hurried his steps. A breeze touched his face, scented with pine and rosemary. He turned to tell Eurydice ...

He stopped himself just in time. Leaning against the cave wall, he clenched his fist. Then he went on.

The cave's narrow way twisted, and he stepped into the full light of the sun. After so long in the dark, he was blinded by the glare, and had to cover his eyes with his arm. The heat of the sun on his skin felt like warm water.

He stepped out of the cave, into the breeze, into the scent of thyme, into bird song. Dizzy with relief and gladness, he raised his arms to the sun and shouted aloud. He had done it; he had outwitted Hades. Hard as it had been, he hadn't looked behind him.

He threw down his lyre and, laughing, turned, holding out his arms.

And saw Eurydice in the shadows of the cave mouth, stretching out her arms to him. She gave one long wild cry as she was snatched back, forever, into the darkness of the Underworld. To live, always, in Hades' hall.

Orpheus had turned too soon. Eurydice had not yet stepped into the sun.

If he had waited one more moment, if he had given her time to take just one more step ...

The Death of Balder

A Viking myth

In Viking mythology, the rainbow is a bridge.
At one end is the Earth, the home of men.
At the other is Asgard, the home of the gods.

In Asgard, there are many halls:

- **Valhalla**: home of Odin, chief god.
  The warriors killed in battle go to
  Valhalla, to join the army Odin is raising
  to fight against the giants at the end of
  the world.
- **Bilskirnir**: home of Thor, the god of thunder.
- **Fensalir**: home of Frigga, Odin's wife.
- **Breidablik**: home of Balder, the son of Odin
  and Frigga.

- *Valhalla:* (say) 'val-ha-luh'.   • *Bilskirnir:* (say) 'bill-skyr-near'.
- *Fensalir:* (say) 'fenn-sa-lear'.   • *Breidablik:* (say) 'bray-da-blik'.

Chapter 1

The nightmare and the promises

 **The most beautiful** hall in Asgard was Breidablik, which means 'broad-gleaming'. Every part of that hall was made with craftsmanship and love. Honesty was built into its very walls, and it was said that no lie could pass through them.

Its owner was Balder, who was tall and beautiful, kind, honest and loyal. He was the most loved of all the gods, by both gods and men.

So when Balder began dreaming of horror and cruelty every night, the gods were worried.

When he dreamed of his own death, the gods were fearful. If no lie could enter Breidablik, then Balder's dreams must tell the truth. He was in danger of death.

None of the gods wanted to lose Balder, but Odin 'all father' dreaded harm to him most of all. He knew that Balder's death would be the beginning of the End of the World.

But none of them – not even Odin, the wisest of them – knew what threatened Balder. It might be anything in the world.

'Then everything in the world must swear a solemn vow that it will not hurt my son,' Frigga said. She left Asgard and crossed the bridge to Earth. She travelled to every part of Man's Home, and asked everything to promise not to harm Balder. Every animal, every bird, every poisonous snake and stinging insect, everything in the sea. Every stone, every kind of metal, every tree, every plant.

Every kind of sickness, every kind of poison, every weapon – she went to every thing that could do harm. She talked, she pleaded. She made them vow that they would never hurt Balder. Most promises were given readily. Balder was much loved. Nothing wished to hurt him.

When Frigga came home to Asgard, she told the gods that she had made Balder safe. They were eager to test whether or not this was true. They all gathered at the feast hall, and Frigga threw a small pebble at her son. It dropped to the ground before it reached him, because all such pebbles had vowed to do him no harm.

The gods threw larger stones, and then knives and axes, but all fell to the ground, keeping their oath and refusing to hurt Balder. Even Thor's great hammer, thrown by Thor, twisted aside and dropped to the ground.

The gods roared with laughter, of joy and relief. It became a game at every gathering, to throw the bones of the feast at Balder, to shoot arrows at him, to throw spears, to stab him with swords, pelt him with stones. Balder laughed through it all, unhurt.

There was a god in Asgard called Loki, the
son of a goddess and a giant. They called him the
Sly One. He loved to cause mischief, to spread
lies, to play tricks. He loved Balder, but hated
him too. To see Balder's beauty made him squint
and scowl. To hear the other gods laugh as they
played their game made him grit his teeth and
rage. He looked round to see if there was any way
he could spoil the game, and he saw Hoder.

Hoder was one of Balder's brothers. But Hoder was blind, and because of that he couldn't take part in the game. He leaned against the wall, listening to the laughter and looking sad. Loki had an idea.

Loki went to Fensalir, Frigga's hall. Outside the door, he spoke a charm and changed his shape. He turned himself into an old woman. Then he went into the hall, asking for food and drink, like a beggar.

'Good luck on the master and mistress!' he said. 'I've wandered a long way – all the road from Man's Home. It'd be good to have a sit and a chat before I go all the way back!'

'Come to the fire,' Frigga said. 'I'll have them bring you bread and ale. Any news?'

'The worlds wag on,' said the old woman. 'One odd thing – in the feasting hall, down the road, they're all throwing stuff at this beautiful man –'

'That's my son, Balder,' Frigga said. 'Don't worry, they can't hurt him.'

'They're throwing axes and spears!'

'But metal won't hurt him, and nor will anything else,' Frigga said.

The old woman marvelled at that and Frigga laughed. She told of her own travels over the wide Earth, and how many things she had begged to take the oath. 'But all things swore not to hurt my son. Nothing on Earth will hurt him.'

'Nothing?' said the old woman.

'Nothing.'

'Nothing at all?'

'Not a single thing.'

'Not even the tiniest beetle, not the smallest mouse, not the least little ...?'

'Nothing,' Frigga said. 'Oh – there is one thing ...'

The old woman kept quiet and waited.

'It's nothing,' said Frigga. 'Such a frail little thing. It couldn't hurt anyone ... So I didn't bother to ask it.'

The old woman kept quiet.

'I mean that little green thing that grows on apple trees and oaks. It's not even a real plant – it can't grow by itself.'

'Mistletoe,' said the old woman.

'That's it,' said Frigga. 'I didn't ask mistletoe. It couldn't hurt Balder anyway, could it?'

'Thank you for your welcome, Lady,' said the old beggar woman. 'Thank you for the food and drink. I have to go now.'

Chapter 2
The fatal dart

As soon as the old woman was outside Fensalir, she turned back into Loki.

Loki, the sly one, crossed the rainbow bridge to Earth. In a grove of oak trees, he found a bunch of mistletoe growing on an oak's trunk. Taking out his knife, he cut it from the tree and carried it back to Asgard. On the way he used his knife to shape the biggest sprig of mistletoe into a dart.

In the feasting hall, the gods still played their game. Hoder still leaned against the wall, listening to the laughter of the other gods. Loki's travel to and from Earth had been swift.

Loki went to Hoder and put his hand on his shoulder. 'You aren't joining in!'

'I'm blind,' said Hoder. 'How can I?'

'Easily, with my help,' Loki said. 'I have a little dart here. I could guide your hand, help you to throw it.'

Hoder smiled.

Loki smiled too. He put the mistletoe dart into Hoder's hand. He took Hoder's hand, and guided him in the throw.

The dart left Hoder's hand, flew through the air, and struck Balder in the chest. It sank into his heart, and Balder fell.

There was silence in the hall. All the gods looked at the fallen Balder. Then they all turned to see where the dart had come from. They saw blind Hoder, and Loki.

'What?' Hoder said. 'What has happened?'

Loki ran away.

The gods and goddesses gathered round Balder. They lifted him up and found that he was dead. Despite all Frigga's efforts, Balder's dreams of death had come true. The puny little mistletoe, the weakest and youngest of all things, had killed a god. There was an outcry of anger and grief. A short while before, the hall had been loud with laughter. Now it was loud with sorrow.

Odin, made no sound, but hid his face in his cloak. Of all the gods, he felt the sharpest stab of sorrow. Balder was his son – but he also knew that Balder's death would bring the End of the World, the Axe Age, the Sword Age, the bitter cold of winter and chaos.

Frigga heard the news and came running, sobbing and crying aloud. She knelt by Balder, and called to him and shook him. When she saw that he was dead, she looked around at all the gods. Still on her knees, she cried out to them, 'Who will win my love and favour? Who will ride into the Underworld for me? Who will go to Hel's Hall and ask her to set Balder free?'

From the crowd of gods, Hermod stepped forward. He was another son of Odin and Frigga, and one of Balder's brothers. He said, 'If Hel can be persuaded to give up my brother, I shall bring him home.'

His father, Odin, said, 'You shall have Sleipnir for the journey.' Sleipnir was Odin's eight-legged dragon-horse, bred from giant-stock. He was the fastest horse alive, and the only one capable of travelling down to the dark roots of the World Tree, to the dark, cold Underworld.

Sleipnir was saddled and bridled and brought to Hermod, who mounted and rode out of Asgard.

• *Hermod*: (say) 'herr-mod'.   • *Sleipnir*: (say) 'slayp-near'.   75

Chapter 3
Balder's funeral

The gods remaining in Asgard held Balder's funeral.

'Bury him in his ship,' Frigga said.

Balder's ship, *Ringhorn*, lay beached on the shore. The gods wanted to launch it, so that it floated level, and then they could build Balder's funeral pyre on board. But the ship was so big and heavy that they couldn't move it from the beach. Even Thor, the strongest of the gods, couldn't heave it from its resting place. All the gods, trying together, couldn't move the great ship.

So messengers were sent into the Giants' Home, to find an ogress named Hyrrokin and to ask for her help.

• *Hyrrokin:* (say) 'hur-rok-kin'.

Hyrrokin came riding to Asgard. Her steed was a huge, bristling wolf. Its bridle and reins were made of living vipers. The ogress leapt from the wolf and strode to the ship. Her wolf – a savage animal – snarled and snapped at those nearest.

The ogress set her shoulder against the ship and braced her feet in the sand. With one strong heave she set *Ringhorn* moving so fast that the wooden rollers beneath its keel burst into flames. The ship groaned as it moved, and the whole world trembled with the shock.

It angered Thor that the ogress should be so careless of the world he strove so hard to protect. He seized his hammer, and would have killed Hyrrokin – except that all the other gods begged for her life.

'She came to help us,' they said.

'It would be dishonourable to kill her.'

'We couldn't have launched the ship without her.'

It was always hard for Thor to control his temper and his hatred of giants, but he gritted his teeth and turned away.

Now the ship was launched, the gods built a pyre on board. Balder's body was laid on the pyre. When Nanna, Balder's wife, saw this, her heart broke and she died. She was laid beside her husband.

Odin wore on his arm the golden ring called Draupnir. He went on board *Ringhorn*, and laid this ring on Balder's chest.

Then the pyre was lit.

All the gods gathered on the shore to watch *Ringhorn* burn. The ice giants came too, and a large crowd of ogres and cliff trolls.

They watched the sailing of *Ringhorn*, its blazing in flames and its sinking.

• *Nanna:* (say) 'nahn-nah'. • *Draupnir:* (say) 'drowp-near'.

Chapter 4

Hermod's quest

Hermod rode on eight-legged Sleipnir. He rode
out of Asgard, out of Man's World and down to
the Underworld, which is found beneath one of
the World Tree's three roots.

For nine nights he rode down through a valley
so deep and dark, he could see nothing. Around
him, he could hear the rushing of the rivers that
spring from beneath the World Tree. Sleipnir
was a bold horse. Carrying Hermod, he pressed
on and crossed all those deep, cold rivers.

trouble, but he was clever and knew a lot.

Crow said, 'I think Eagle-hawk is right about Cockatoo being dead, and that his spirit's gone away to another place. But I don't agree that he'll never come back. Because I think death is like this ...' And Crow picked up a stick of wood and threw it into the river.

The animals watched it fall into the water and vanish, just as the stone had – but then it bobbed up again, because wood floats. 'Cockatoo's spirit has gone into another place,' said Crow, 'just as the  stick went under the water. But just as the stick returned from under the water, so Cockatoo's spirit will return from that other place.'

The animals looked at Cockatoo's body. It had been lying there, in the heat, for a while now.

Ants were crawling all over it, and the feathers were bedraggled. 'He'd better hurry up and get back, then,' Quoll said. 'His body's starting to look a bit tatty.'

'Cockatoo's spirit won't come back to this body,' Crow said. 'It'll come back to another body.'

The animals were astonished, and a great noise of argument and talk broke out. This was the first time in the world that there had ever been such an idea. Every animal had something to say about it.

'We must test it!' Numbat said.

'I won't believe it until I see it!' said Wallaby.

'We ought to try out this death,' said Dingo, 'and see what it's like!'

'But who is going to do it?' asked Eagle-hawk. 'Remember, you must leave your body here – your body that you love so much. Your body will not see, or hear, or move, or feel or smell or taste. While your body lies here and rots away, your spirit must find its way into another place. Then it must return – in another body. Is there anyone among us who thinks they can do all this?'

'Cockatoo has!' Wallaby said.

'He hasn't come back,' said Quoll.

'Ah, but would we know if he had?' asked Crow. 'He would have come back in another shape.'

'As another Cockatoo?' Wallaby asked.

'Who knows? He might have come back as a fish – or a gum tree!'

The animals all started shouting for Cockatoo, and going up to gum trees and crocodiles and even stones, and asking them, 'Are you Cockatoo?'

Chapter 2
The test

When the animals couldn't find Cockatoo,
they all came back to the shade of the big gum
tree. Eagle-hawk and the other elders were
waiting there.

'Are we going to try death?' Eagle-hawk asked.
'If so, who's going to do it?'

The goanna, the wombat, the possum and
the snake came forward. 'We think we can do it,'
Snake said.

'Yes, we've made up our minds, we're going to
die this winter,' said Possum.

'Winters are miserable anyway,' said Wombat. 'Dying will make a change.'

'Right,' said Goanna. 'You lot can all meet us here next spring – to give us a cheer when we all show up from the other place in our new bodies.'

The other animals agreed to this. They knew when the different seasons were coming by watching the way the stars changed in the sky.

All through the winter the animals watched the skies, waiting for spring. Everyone was always eager for spring, but that year they longed for it even more than usual. The animals started their journey to the river bank early, because everyone wanted to be sure they got a good place.

When the first days of spring arrived, the river banks were already crowded with animals, all waiting to find out what had happened to Snake, Goanna, Wombat and Possum. How would they know their old friends, they asked? Would they give them a special sign? Would Wombat come as a possum, and Snake as a wombat, and Possum as a goanna ...?

Then, along the banks came Goanna, Possum, Snake and Wombat. They looked just as they always did, except that they were all weak and thin, and tottered as they came. Snake's skin hung half off him, in rags and tatters. Possum and Wombat's fur was lumpy, straggly, and full of dust and dirt. The other animals didn't cheer. They watched in silence.

When Goanna, Wombat, Snake and Possum had taken their places in the shadow of the gum tree, Wallaby said, 'What happened? You all look terrible!'

'Well, we have been dead,' said Wombat.

'I don't think I'll try it,' said Platypus.

'It wasn't so bad,' Goanna said. 'Is there anything to eat? I'm starving.'

Eagle-hawk said, 'I don't think you have been dead at all.'

'What?' cried Possum. 'We haven't seen or heard or moved or spoken all winter. What's that, if not death?'

'But you haven't changed your bodies,'

Crow said. 'Except that Snake has shaken off half his skin. But that's not enough. You haven't been dead.'

'We went away into another place,' said Goanna.

'Tell me exactly what you did,' said Crow.

'I slithered into a little hole,' said Snake, 'and hid, so I'd have peace and quiet while I died.'

'I went down into my burrow, where it's nice and warm,' said Wombat. 'I thought if I was going to die, I might as well make myself comfortable.'

Goanna stood up on his back legs and said, 'I dug a hole to die in too. I like digging holes. But I died, I'm sure of it.'

'What about you, Possum?' Crow asked.

'I made myself a snug little nest out of leaves and grass,' Possum said.

'And you went to sleep,' said Crow. 'You were all sleeping, not dead at all.'

'But you've got to start somewhere,' Goanna said. 'You can't be dead straight off, just like that.

We thought we'd ease into it.'

'Cockatoo did it straight off,' said Bandicoot. 'He fell out of a tree and wallop! He was dead, no messing.'

'Maybe he'd been practising on the quiet,' Goanna said. 'We don't know.'

'Sleeping isn't death,' Crow said. 'Nowhere near. Goanna, Wombat, Snake, Possum – thank you for trying, but you've nothing to tell us about dying.'

'Still, it was a good way to pass the winter,' Wombat said.

'Too right,' said Goanna. 'I've never liked winters.' And from that day to this, Wombat, Goanna, Snake and Possum sleep away the winter.

'We still don't know about death,' said Eagle-hawk. 'How are we going to find out?'

No one had any ideas.

'How did Cockatoo do it?' Wallaby asked. 'He's the only one who knows. Did anyone see how he did it?'

'We told you,' said Galah. 'He fell out of
a tree.'

'But that's not enough! Lots of us have fallen
out of trees without dying. He must have done
something else. What?'

Animals were shaking their heads. No
one knew.

'Come on, you cockatoos,' Koala said.
'You must know. How's it done?'

But the cockatoos all flapped and screeched
and screamed. 'Don't look at us!'

'We don't know!'

'We had nothing to do with it!'

A little voice spoke from the gum tree.
'Let us try!'

Eagle-hawk looked closely at the tree and saw a caterpillar. Lots of caterpillars. On the tree-trunk, in the leaves, on the twigs, in the grass, were hundreds of tiny grubs and bugs, all shouting, 'We'll do it! Let us try!'

The animals all laughed, because the bugs and grubs were so small and ugly. If Wombat, Goanna, Snake and Possum couldn't solve the mystery, what made the grubs think they could? They were silly, crawling, ignorant little things.

'Don't laugh – we know how to do it!' a caterpillar squeaked. But the animals laughed louder and longer. An ugly little caterpillar couldn't be good at anything, let alone something so difficult.

Eagle-hawk felt sorry for the grubs, and said, 'No one should be laughed at just because they're small and have many legs. Let them try.'

To the grubs and bugs, he said, 'Do your best, and we'll all meet here again next spring, to see what you've discovered.'

Chapter 3
The changes

The animals spent all summer making jokes about what fools the grubs and bugs were going to look. Songs were made up about how ugly the grubs were, and how they tried to die, but couldn't even get to sleep, as Wombat and the others had.

'Look at me, I'm a dead caterpillar!' said Kookaburra, and then made loud snoring noises. The animals laughed until they were almost sick.

The bugs and grubs had to listen to it every day.

At summer's end, the animals all left the river, calling out that they would see each other next spring. 'But we won't see the caterpillars – they'll be dead!' And there was more laughter.

What did the bugs and grubs do? The water bugs wrapped themselves in fine, thin sheets of bark and threw themselves into the river. Other bugs burrowed under the bark of trees, and some buried themselves in the earth. All of them took themselves from this place, to another place.

Winter passed, and the bugs and grubs stayed hidden.

The stars moved across the sky, and spring came again. The animals gathered at the river. But no bugs or grubs came.

'They're dead, of course,' said the animals, and laughed.

That night, as the animals sat around their campfires, dragonflies flew into the firelight, crowds of them, their wings sparkling with every colour. 'We come as messengers!' they said.

'Tomorrow our cousins will return from death in their new bodies!'

That started more gossip around the fires. The animals were too excited to sleep. Even the plants heard about it, and in their excitement, they flowered. The wattle threw up masses of bright yellow flowers, and the waratah burst out with a brilliant red. That was the first time the plants had ever flowered. They looked so fresh and new, no one can possibly imagine how beautiful it seemed to all the animals.

As the sun rose, the dragonflies appeared again, their wings shimmering. Behind them came something never seen before. Behind them came a flight, a wave, of yellow butterflies, dancing, darting, fluttering. The animals stood astonished, gaping – and then, behind the yellow butterflies, came a mass, a crowd, of red butterflies, like flying fire-sparks.

Then came blue butterflies, blue as the sky, blue as water.

Then green butterflies, jade green, moon green. More butterflies and more, of every colour.

The animals had never seen a single butterfly before, they all cried out in a great bellow of wonder at the delicacy, the dancing, the colour.

The birds were so amazed that they sang.

That was the first time in the world that birds ever sang.

Oh, that Dreamtime morning ... the land was covered, as it had never been before, with yellow and red flowers. The air was filled, as it had never been before, by birdsong. And a sight never seen before: thousands of butterflies dancing.

No morning before or since has ever been so beautiful or so full of wonders as that Dreamtime morning.

The butterflies, blue and red and green and yellow, fluttered about the heads of Crow, Eagle-hawk and the other animals. 'We left our bodies in this place,' they said, 'and our spirits went away to another place, and now we've returned, in new bodies. Have we done death?'

111

'Not quite, little ones,' said Eagle-hawk. 'But you have shown us what death is like. You have changed from one thing to another. And for that, we shall always honour you.'

* * *

If you doubt this story, just look about you. Every winter the snake, the possum, the wombat and the goanna go away to sleep, just as they first did in the Dreamtime.

And every winter the little grubs wrap themselves up and bury themselves; and every spring brings butterflies, flowers and birdsong.

We have flowers, and birdsong, and butterflies, all because of that first death.

Death is like another change of season – not the end, but a new start.